PROFILE
of the 47s

Plate 1 (Previous Page): Running through the attractive tree-lined cutting on the western approaches to Bournemouth Station, on 6th September 1984, with the 14.40 Poole to Liverpool (Lime Street) train, Class 47/4 No. 47501 slows for the first scheduled stop of a journey that specifies calls at Southampton, Winchester, Basingstoke, Reading, Oxford, Banbury, Leamington Spa, Birmingham (New Street), Wolverhampton, Stafford and Runcorn, before being due to arrive at Liverpool at 20.49 — a journey time of over six hours. This locomotive was repainted in Inter-City sector livery at Old Oak Common, February 1987.

Plate 2 (Above): Due to realignment of track taking place on the fast lines through Rugby on the weekend of 11th/12th April 1981, a number of special trains operated between Paddington and Wolverhampton via Banbury, in addition to scheduled Birmingham line services, in place of the usual electrically-powered trains from Euston. Most of the services were entrusted to Class 47s, such as this one leaving Harbury Tunnel behind No. 47468.

PROFILE
of the 47s

Plate 3. Travelling high above the Cornish countryside on St. Pinnock Viaduct, Class 47/0 No. 47011 has an easy time hauling just two Crosfield tanks that make up the 09.35 St Blazey to Warrington freight, on 1st October 1985. In March 1987 this locomotive was stopped at its home depot of Bescot with problems and subsequently withdrawn from service.

Brian Morrison

Oxford Publishing Company

Plate 4: Entering Horbury Cutting at Healey Mills, Wakefield, on 5th September 1980, Class 47/3 No. 47373 heads eastwards with a merry-go-round coal train, this being one of the class fitted with slow speed control, allowing the driver to set a steady 5m.p.h. for the m.g.r. loading and unloading processes. This locomotive has the added refinement of remote slow speed control and a flashing blue lamp on the cab dome, as shown in close-up in the inset.

ISBN 0 86093 240 0

A FOULIS-OPC Railway Book

Published by:
Haynes Publishing Group
Sparkford, Near Yeovil, Somerset BA22 7JJ

Haynes Publication Inc.
861 Lawrence Drive, Newbury Park, California 91320, USA.

British Library Cataloguing in Publication Data
Morrison, Brian
    Profile of the 47's
    1. Class 47 (Diesel locomotive) —
    Pictorial works
    I. Title
    625.2'622'0941   TJ619.4.G7
    ISBN 0-86093-240-0

Library of Congress catalog card number
87-82235

Introduction

Seven years have elapsed since I had the pleasure of compiling *The Power of the 47s* and, without doubt, more has happened to the fleet in this period than took place in the previous eighteen years. Conversion for electric train heating carries on apace, headlamps have been fitted in addition to the front marker lights, more 'push-pull' Part 7s have been added to the ScotRail fleet, the experimental Part 6 locomotive became a Class 58 engined Part 9, well over one hundred of the class are now named, and differing liveries abound from Network SouthEast, Inter-City and ScotRail through to Railfreight and GWR lined green. The fleet's territory has also extended and examples of the class can now be seen from Penzance to Inverness and from Angelsey to East Anglia. They are the mainstays of the Inter-City Cross London services, the Glasgow to Edinburgh high speed trains, and the Highland main line traffic, and can be observed on a myriad of duties, almost throughout the length and breadth of the British Rail system.

With the original members of the fleet having been in use for some twenty-five years, it was obvious that the first withdrawals were imminent, and this has proved to be the case. It was, in fact, 1962 when the first of a fleet to number over 500 locomotives appeared from the Falcon Works of the Brush Group of Companies at Loughborough constructed in collaboration with the British Transport Commission.

Specifications required utilisation of the Sulzer 12LDA28 diesel engine, which had been successfully tested up to 2,750b.h.p. and a body mounted on a Co-Co wheel arrangement. The British Rail workshops at Crewe later gave a hand with the building, but the majority of the machines emanated from Loughborough. Originally known as Brush/Sulzer Type 4s, they became Class 47s under the BR locomotive classification scheme of the early 1970s, with the standard Class 47/0 being fitted with steam heating facilities, the 47/3s having no heating provision, and the 47/4s having electric or dual heating. In reality many of the steam heat boilers were isolated through the years and the 'standard' locomotive of the class is now the Part 4 variety, into which category many of the 47/0s have been converted.

The ninety six pages of this album contain nearly 200 photographs of the class on every type of train, captured throughout the BR network and is, I hope, a fitting tribute to the largest fleet of main line diesel locomotives ever constructed in this country.

Brian Morrison
Sidcup, Kent
1987

Note: All photographs contained in this album that are not otherwise credited were taken by the author.

Plate 5 (Below): Skirting the North Sea at Nigg Bay, south of Aberdeen, on 19th April 1984, one of the many Class 47s allocated to Glasgow (Eastfield) Depot, No. 47141 (now 47614), nears journey's end with the 09.35 service from Glasgow (Queen Street) to Aberdeen.

1960s — The Early Days

Under Construction

Plate 8: No. D1731 (47550) was the 100th Type 4 diesel locomotive manufactured by Brush at Loughborough, and is shown here in process of delivery to British Railways in June 1964.

Brush Electrical Engineering

Plate 6 (Above Left): A general view photographed inside Crewe Works in 1964 showing some 18 Brush Type 4s under construction. The design dispensed with a conventional underframe, the whole of the body, excluding the cabs, being built as a fully load bearing structure on monocoque principles.

Colin J. Marsden Collection

Plate 7 (left): The Falcon Works of Brush Electrical Engineering constructed over 300 Type 4s between 1962 and May 1968 when the last locomotive, No. D1961 (47515) eventually appeared. In this view, from inside the Falcon Works, Loughborough, two of the fleet receive final touches prior to delivery to British Rail.

Colin J. Marsden Collection

Plate 9: Constructed in December 1964, No. D1639 (47055/47652) has rectifications undertaken to the power unit in Crewe Works yard on 11th March 1965 prior to delivery. The twin-banked Sulzer engines had a number of teething problems from new and, between 1966 and 1969, they were all effectively derated from the original 2,650b.h.p. to 2,580b.h.p. which still applies today. The view also includes a BR Standard 9F 2-10-0 steam engine shown to the rear.

Colin J. Marsden Collection

Early Workings

Plate 10: The 07.55 departure from Leamington Spa (General) for Birkenhead leaves Solihull on 8th April 1964 powered by No. D1700 (47112). To the rear, Standard Class 4MT 2-6-4T No. 80072 steams freely with the 07.45 Leamington Spa to Birmingham (Snow Hill) local train which is running on the relief line.

Michael Mensing

Plate 11: Passing a surviving Great Northern Railway somersault signal at the closed station of Littleworth, Lincolnshire, on the Peterborough to Spalding line, on 18th June 1966, No. D1791 (47310) has charge of a haul of empty coal wagons.

Michael Mensing

Plate 12: A southbound parcels turn is pictured north of Ludlow, on 7th August 1965, headed by No. D1676 (47090/ 47623) prior to receiving its name of *Vulcan.* Twelve of the class built at Crewe were given names of this type appertaining to creatures of great strength.

Michael Mensing

Plate 13: Passing the site of Hayles Abbey Halt on the Cheltenham to Stratford-on-Avon line, on 18th June 1966, No. D1674 (47088/47653) *Samson* hauls the 14.30 Paignton to Wolverhampton (Low Level) service taking South Devon holiday-makers back home to the Midlands. The work-stained condition of the locomotive has almost obliterated its original two-tone green livery which would, otherwise, have contrasted nicely with the all-maroon stock.

Michael Mensing

Plate 14: With a Denparts wagon bringing up the rear, a short parcels train heads for Harbury Tunnel on the 'Birmingham Direct' line on 21st June 1966, providing an easy task for No. D1720 (47129/47658).

Michael Mensing

Plate 15: Less than two months since delivery from Brush at Loughborough, No. D1710 (47121) approaches Solihull, on 16th March 1964, with the 07.25 express from Wolverhampton (Low Level) to Paddington.

Michael Mensing

Plate 16: A rare photograph of No. D1733 (47141/47614) in experimental pale blue livery with small bodyside numbers at either end in place of the normal cabside ones. This locomotive was specifically prepared for the XP64 prototype passenger train of 1964 and, originally, had the new BR logo on a square red panel beneath the cab windows, this eventually being placed centrally on each body side without the red background, and the numbers returned to their original location below the cabside windows. Although the corporate 'Rail Blue' colour to be chosen for all BR locomotives and stock was darker than this, No.D1733 was, nevertheless, the precursor of BR's blue livery era. Arriving at Knowle & Dorridge Station on Sunday, 2nd May 1965, the locomotive is seen hauling the 15.20 Wolverhampton (Low Level) to Paddington train.

Michael Mensing

Plate 17: With the 'D' prefix now removed from the locomotive number, No. 1903 (47227) heads a merry-go-round coal train from Betteshanger Colliery, in Kent, at Aberthaw Power Station in South Glamorgan, this locomotive being one of some seventy of the type fitted with slow-speed control for this type of work.

Colin J. Marsden Collection

Plate 18: No. D1849 (47199) approaches Carlisle (Citadel) Station on 26th May 1967 with an 'up' Freightliner. Of all the liveries to be carried by the fleet of Brush Type 4s over the ensuing years, the original two-tone green, devised specifically for them by design consultants Wilkes & Ashmore, was probably the most attractive as the centre band of light green nicely disguised their otherwise rather plain, slab-sided appearance.

Martin Welch

Plate 19: Returning to the Severn Valley Railway after exhibition at Tyseley, Birmingham, No. D1723 (47132/47540) has been adorned with large new-style BR logos at each end of the body sides. In this view, photographed on 29th September 1969 at Bewdley, the locomotive is hauling preserved Ivatt 2-6-0 No. 46443 and Collett 0-6-0 No. 3205 as, at this time, the Severn Valley Railway had only achieved running powers from Bridgnorth to Hampton Loade.

John Vaughan

Plate 20: With the advent of computerisation for British Rail, their TOPS programme (Total Operations Processing System) introduced class numbers for the various locomotive types extant at that time, and the Brush/Sulzer Type 4s became known as Class 47s. Renumbering went ahead apace, and during the period of change it was possible to observe green-liveried members of the class with new numbers, while a number of the blue ones still retained the pre-TOPS variety. On 12th June 1974, No. 47418, in recently out-shopped condition, departs from Darlington hauling the 17.23 Newcastle to King's Cross Inter-City working.

Plate 21: Traversing the 'slow' line through Sonning Cutting on 27th April 1974, No. 47508 heads an 'up' Inter-City service for Paddington. In 1979, this locomotive received the name *Great Britain,* but this was changed to *S.S. Great Britain* as a part of the 'GWR 150' celebrations of 1985.

Plate 22: On 12th September 1973, No. 1533 (47425 *Holbeck*) emerges from Copenhagen Tunnel and commences the climb of Holloway Bank to Finsbury Park with the 16.25 King's Cross to Cleethorpes service. Note the wide open Serck hydraulically-operated radiator grilles on the lower portion of the roof behind the cab. Controlled by the radiator-housed thermostat, the type was fitted from 1965 to replace the original fixed-aperture triple panel variety illustrated by examples seen in *Plates 10, 11, 14, 15 and 16.*

Plate 23: Although allocated the number 47062 on TOPS, this identification was never carried as the locomotive was converted to supply electric train heating prior to the renumbering taking place, and had to be numbered into the 47/4 category. Carrying its new identification of 47545 on 11th July 1976, the locomotive departs from Nottingham with the 10.50 train for London (St. Pancras).

John F. Henton

Plate 24: The widespread utilisation of visual displays fitted in power signal boxes was to bring about the demise of train identification numbers being displayed in the route indicator panels that were constructed for this purpose. Code 1N28 signified that this train was the 13.30 Liverpool Street to Norwich Inter-City express which, on 25th June 1975, approached its destination behind No. 47010.

Plate 25: Passing under Ranelagh Bridge on the approaches to Paddington Station, on 21st May 1975, No. 47068 (47632) is rostered for the 14.25 Birmingham (New Street) to Paddington service, and displays the appropriate headcode of 1V48. To the left, two others of the class wait in the sidings prior to their next duty, accompanied by a Class 50 locomotive.

Plate 26: High above the River Tweed, No. 47528 crosses the massive Royal Border Bridge into Berwick-upon-Tweed, on 14th December 1974, hauling the 07.15 York to Aberdeen train (1S51). As No. D1111, this locomotive was the very last to be completed at Crewe, in February 1967.

Plate 27: The first number displayed in the indicator panels signified the type of train that was in tow — the letter indicated the district, division or region of the train's destination, and the final two characters the reporting number of the service. The letter 'Z' was used for specials, such as this example, the 18.50 summer extra from Paignton to Glasgow (Central), seen here arriving as empty coaching stock from Goodrington carriage sidings, Paignton, on 2nd August 1975 in the charge of No. 47488.

Plate 28 (Left): At speed through Potters Bar Cutting on 6th December 1975, No. 47526 powers the 08.50 Inter-City express from York to King's Cross, identified by the code 1A09. The number of similar looking trains that passed here, coupled with timings that were sometimes a little awry, meant that without the headcode train identification for anyone outside a signal box would be somewhat uncertain.

Plate 29 (Below Left): The long, straight section of line between York and Northallerton has long been utilised for high speed running. Hammering through the Yorkshire countryside at Pilmoor, south of Thirsk, on 13th June 1974, No. 47457 powers the 13.00 King's Cross to Edinburgh Inter-City express, timed to arrive in the Scottish capital at 19.50, with stops at Doncaster, York, Darlington, Durham, Newcastle and Berwick-upon-Tweed. With the same number of stops, the Inter-City 125 High Speed Trains that now operate this service cover the distance in under five hours.

Plate 30 (Below): A low wintery sun highlights the masonry of the Royal Border Bridge at Berwick-upon-Tweed, and glints from the flanks of both locomotive and train as No. 47410 accelerates southwards with the 10.06 Edinburgh to York Inter-City service, on 14th December 1974. This locomotive was withdrawn from service in May 1987 having been in service for more than 24 years.

Plate 32 (Above): The 14.50 service from Inverness to Glasgow (Queen Street) passes Blair Atholl on 31st May 1977 headed by No. 47006. The locomotive's silver roof betrays the fact that this was a Stratford (London) machine very far from 'home' at the time.

Plate 31 (Left): Having been through works quite recently, No. 47209 was in good order both externally and internally on 24th March 1974, and runs the 13.10 Glasgow (Queen Street) to Aberdeen Sunday service through Nigg Bay Cutting, south of Craiginches, some ten minutes early.

Plate 33 (below): Climbing the 1 in 96 gradient between Aberdeen and Ferryhill, on 8th December 1974, No. 47470 travels under the maze of semaphore signals that were in existence southwards from the 'Granite City' at this time, and passes Ferryhill signal box with the 'up' 'Sunday Aberdonian' for Kings Cross. This locomotive was named *University of Edinburgh* in July 1983.

Plate 34 (Above Left): On a crisp March evening in 1974, No. 47053 races through the Scottish countryside near Drumlithie powering the 16.23 express from Aberdeen to York. The low lighting illuminates the underframe of the locomotive, where the tanks for the train heating boiler water and fuel oil can clearly be seen underhung between the bogies.

Plate 35 (Left): The 'up' 'Aberdonian' for King's Cross is restarted from a misty Montrose on 30th March 1974 by No. 1975 (47517 *Andrew Carnegie*) and prepares to cross the Montrose Basin.

Plate 36 (Above): Despite the weak sunshine that is apparent, the temperature at Aberdeen on 11th November 1973 when this photograph was taken was well below zero and, in addition, a freezing gale-force wind was blowing in from the North Sea. On one of the few exposures taken by the author that day, No. 1513 (47414) waits for the scheduled time of departure with the 12.20 Sunday service for London (King's Cross). This locomotive was withdrawn in March 1986.

Freight Movements

Plate 37 (Left): Heading a Freightliner for Southampton on 27th April 1974, No. 47020 (47556) is about to pass under the Bournemouth line that is carried by Battledown Flyover at Worting Junction, south of Basingstoke. The square works plate below the cab window signifies that this locomotive was constructed at Crewe; the Brush-manufactured types having an oval plate.

Plate 38 (Below Left): On 12th June 1974, a heavy Anglo-Scottish 'Chrysler UK' container train, heading for Linwood, climbs Shap Fell powered by No. 47469, since named *Glasgow Chamber of Commerce.*

Plate 39 (Below): Although not yet mid-afternoon, the first signs of nightfall were already apparent at Aberdeen on 10th September 1974 as No. 47144 heads south with a train of fish wagons that had emanated from Fraserburgh. With the Fraserburgh line now closed, this traffic now utilises road transport.

Route Indicator Panels — R.I.P.!

Plate 40: Between the time that train identification numbers were phased out and marker-light panels installed in their place, the indicator panels on nearly all of the Class 47 fleet were set permanently at '0000', and the selector and operating handles were removed. With the first blind having vibrated round to a '1', No. 47156 rolls into Colchester Station on 11th May 1977 hauling the 11.30 Liverpool Street to Norwich Inter-City service.

Plate 41: Night falls at Stranraer Harbour Station on 2nd June 1977 as the 22.00 overnight service for Euston prepares to depart behind No. 47466. With the old line eastwards to Dumfries, via Newton Stewart and Castle Douglas, having closed many years ago, trains from Stranraer are now obliged to travel north to Ayr and Kilmarnock before turning south again for Dumfries and Carlisle, a round trip of 166½ miles.

Plate 42: An 'up' train is powered through Marston Green Station, between Lea Hall and Birmingham International, on 6th October 1979, by No. 47402, since named *Gateshead*. Without the assistance given by a route indicator panel, identification of the train was not possible.

Plate 43: On 16th October 1976, No. 47136 (47621 *Royal County of Berkshire*) storms away from the mandatory Oxford stop with the 14.05 Paddington to Birmingham (New Street) service. Part of the fuelling facilities available here at this time are shown on the right, together with the floodlighting provided.

Plate 44 (Above): The 'Rail Blue' livery that was standard for all BR locomotives for approaching two decades was mundane at best but, when work-stained, it took on a decidedly grubby appearance, as shown with No. 47418 arriving at St. Albans (City) Station with the 07.55 Sheffield (Midland) to St Pancras train, on the equally grubby day of 14th January 1978.

Plate 46 (Top Right): On the sunny morning of 26th February 1977, No. 47105 takes a rake of ten Mk.I coaches out of Paddington Station forming a Millwall Football Club 'Footex' special to Plymouth. The train is on the slow line, and passing the London Transport platforms of Royal Oak Station to the rear.

Plate 45 (Below): Freshly painted bodywork provides a much brighter look to No. 47216, seen crossing the River Exe out of Exeter (St. David's) Station on 13th July 1976 hauling an Edinburgh to Plymouth cross-country service. A strange story attaches to this particular locomotive. Seemingly a clairvoyant had a premonition that a locomotive numbered 47216 would be involved in an accident resulting in loss of life and, in 1981, notified British Rail accordingly. Presumably on the premise that it is better to be safe than sorry, British Rail actually arranged for the number to be changed to a vacant one in the fleet, No. 47299. During early 1984, however, No. 47299 was seriously damaged in an accident with a diesel multiple unit that involved loss of life!

Plate 47 (Left): In teeming rain, on 28th May 1976, No. 47433 comes off the Tay Bridge at Wormit hauling the 16.20 Aberdeen to York Inter-City service.

Plate 48 (Below): Oil tanks from both Thameshaven and Coryton oil refineries are assembled in Ripple Lane yards, Barking, from where they are made up into various trains for many parts of the BR network. Prior to leaving with some 24 tanks in tow, No. 47192 engages in a spot of shunting, on 31st October 1979.

Plate 49: Notching up from the usual Reading stop, No. 47103 heads for the Midlands, on 7th April 1976, with the 16.05 Paddington to Birmingham (New Street) train, and passes a Class 08 0-6-0 shunter engaged in shunting duties on the left.

Plate 50: Heading the 07.40 from Aberdeen, No. 47038 (47564) bursts from Queen Street Tunnel into Glasgow (Queen Street) Station on 2nd June 1977, having made the journey in just under three hours. In January 1987 this locomotive received the nameplates *Colossus* from No. 47641 which had been re-named *Fife Region*.

Marker Lights and Variations

Plate 51: With the route indicator panels plated over, and marker lights inserted into a black background, No. 47119 leaves Didcot, on 1st March 1979, hauling the return 'Paddington Anniversary Special' after the failure of the rostered steam locomotive. This was now to be the standard appearance for the majority of the fleet until the time when the present day yellow panels and headlights became the norm.

Plate 52: Even from the very early days of fitting marker lights there were some variances and, for some unknown reason, No. 47014 sports blue ones. On 11th May 1977, the locomotive arrives at Colchester, heading the 10.32 Norwich to Liverpool Street service.

Plate 53: Rather more akin to eyes than marker lights, No. 47015 displays this variety at Perth, on 2nd June 1978, whilst on empty coaching stock duties.

John Chalcraft

Plate 54: The Stratford trade mark of silver roof panels has an added touch with No. 47460, as the marker light background has been painted yellow to match the rest of the locomotive's front end. On 11th September 1978, it has been commandeered for East Coast Main Line duties, and emerges from Gasworks Tunnel into King's Cross with the 09.00 Inter-City service from Aberdeen. At a time when Stratford had no allocation of named locomotives, two plates were made up and affixed unofficially to this machine, which for a few weeks became *Great Eastern*. This move appeared to precipitate some action from upon high, as shortly afterwards a number of names were bestowed upon Stratford's Class 47 fleet including the name *Great Eastern* for No. 47169 (47581).

Plate 55: With a barrier wagon between itself and the haul of bogie chemical tanks in tow, No. 47041 (47630) passes Melton Ross, near Barnetby, on 1st September 1979, heading for Immingham.

Plate 56: Winter lighting can be particulary beautiful, lending a somewhat brittle, golden effect to locomotive and stock. Unfortunately this situation only applies when there is a portion of metalwork that is capable of some form of reflective property! A begrimed No. 47531 bursts from Elstree Tunnel, in Hertfordshire, on 11th February 1978, powering the 12.01 Inter-City train from St. Pancras to Sheffield.

Plate 57: On an otherwise cloudy 31st May 1977, a lucky flash of sunshine serves to highlight the 18.45 Edinburgh to Aberdeen express, crossing the Tay Bridge behind No. 47158 (now 47634 *Henry Ford*).

Plate 58: Consisting of a rake of Mk.II Inter-City stock, and complete with a buffet car, empty coaching stock of a 'Merrymaker' excursion that had earlier terminated at Marylebone is removed by the train locomotive No 47496 (now 47710 *Sir Walter Scott*). Passing London Transport third rail at West Hampstead, on 16th September 1978, the e.c.s. is heading for Willesden carriage sidings, where it will stay until needed for the return journey — an unusual stretch of line over which to see a Class 47 operating.

Plate 59: An 'up' train of Algeco tanks is hurried down-grade towards Brentwood, Essex, on 19th May 1977, having run down from Ingrave Summit on the fast line, powered by Class 47/3 No. 47326, which is fitted with similar marker lights to the ones illustrated *in Plate 53.*

Plate 60: Passing Pyle, near Bridgend, on 13th September 1979, No. 47254 (47651) heads chemical tanks westwards, and has no time to waste with only a short working pathway between passing Inter-City 125s.

Plate 61: With the sunshine breaking through a heavy overnight fog, No. 47298 brings a rake of heavy bogie oil tanks through Southall, Middlesex, on 20th March 1976, heading for Acton yards, from where they will eventually return to Ripple Lane and Coryton oil terminal.

Plate 62 (Below): The town in the background of this view is Porthleven, and when this photograph was taken, on 5th March 1979, its inhabitants had no idea that they were to have a station of their own again nearly thirty years after losing their existing one in June 1956. When this photograph was taken, however, all trains thundered through the town on the last few miles into Aberdeen, as with No. 47516 (now No. 47708 *Waverley*) hauling the 10.45 service from Edinburgh.

Plate 63 (Above Right): The Southern Region have only ever had one small allocation of Class 47s, which was between 1966 and 1968 when Nos. D1921 – D1926 (47244 – 47249) were transferred to Eastleigh Depot for working a number of duties that included expresses to Bournemouth and boat trains to Weymouth. They were, however, replaced by the Class 74 electro-diesel rebuilds and returned to the Western Region. Of course the class still visit the 'Southern' on innumerable occasions, and are nearly as common in third rail territory as Stewarts Lane's own fleet of Class 33s. At Southampton Station, on 13th May 1978, No. 47143 has charge of the 08.50 Weymouth to Leeds cross-country service, whilst a Class 33/0 locomotive passes through with a special from Southampton West Docks to Waterloo.

Plate 64 (Right): Precursors of today's cross-London Inter-City services, the Brighton to Manchester trains, have, in fact, been using the West London line through Kensington Olympia for many years, although passengers have not had the use of the station. On 9th May 1979, No. 47446 threads Clapham Cutting with the morning northbound service.

Plate 65: On 22nd August 1979, No. 47111 heads down the Dartford Loop line, between Mottingham and New Eltham, hauling a load of stone hoppers towards Hoo Junction. This locomotive was involved in a serious accident with a diesel multiple unit at Preston early in 1986, and was subsequently condemned as beyond economical repair, being moved to Cardiff (Canton) Depot for cutting up a month later, where it provided spares for the Canton allocation of Class 47s, particularly with regard to bogies.

Plate 66: The low February sunshine provides pleasant lighting for photography, but does little to warm the air at Micheldever as No. 47474 approaches the station with the 09.42 cross-country service from Poole to Leeds and Newcastle.

Plate 67: With the skyscrapers of Croydon on the horizon, No. 47508 (now named *S.S. Great Britain*) returns 'light engine' to Acton, having dropped off the morning coal train in Norwood Yard. To the right, a Class 415/2 4EPB electric multiple unit, No. 5361, forms the 12.23 West Croydon to London (Victoria) stopping train and, in the distance, the yards of Selhurst Depot contain, among other things, a Class 33/2 Bo-Bo and a Class 73 electro-diesel on an 'up' freight.

Plate 68: On 13th May 1978, No. 47247 (47650) bustles through Lyndhurst Road Station, in Hampshire's New Forest, with the 07.55 Leeds to Weymouth service.

1980s — Decade of Change

Push-Pull

Plate 69 (Left): Sixteen Scottish-based members of the Class 47 fleet have been converted for a special push-pull system of operation for the Edinburgh to Glasgow high-speed services, where the trains are propelled in one direction utilising a specially converted Driving Brake Open Second, and hauled in the normal way in the other. The small fleet are classified as 47/7, and often wander from their intended route as with No. 47710 *Sir Walter Scott* passing Ferryhill, Aberdeen, on 19th April 1982, with the 07.35 Glasgow (Queen Street) to Aberdeen express. These were the first of the fleet to be fitted with headlights as standard but, at this time, they were not standard headlights, being of the round variety.

Plate 71 (Right): The DBSOs that form the 'other end' of the hourly push-pull services between Scotland's two major cities were converted from Mk.IIf Brake Open Seconds, with part of the brake section being converted into a driving cab. Powered at the rear by a Class 47/7, one such vehicle heads the 11.30 Edinburgh to Glasgow (Queen Street) train near Linlithgow, on 29th January 1981.

Plate 72 (Right): On the same day, No. 47706 *Holyrood* fairly hurtles the 11.00 Glasgow (Queen Street) to Edinburgh express through Old Philipstown, near Linlithgow.

Plate 70 (Left): Recently out-shopped from BREL Crewe, No. 47709 *The Lord Provost* prepares to leave Glasgow (Queen Street) Station, on 28th May 1980, with the 13.00 Inter-City service for Edinburgh.

George C. O'Hara

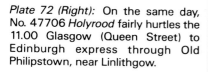

Lines from Liverpool Street

Plate 73: No. 47579 *James Nightall, G.C.* powers the 13.30 Liverpool Street to Norwich Inter-City train, and approaches Stratford Station on 8th November 1983. The glowing marker lights testify to the drabness of the weather.

Plate 74: On the same afternoon, No. 47075 (now No. 47645 *Robert F. Fairlie*) hauls a block loading of 'Tilbury Roadstone' hoppers through Stratford Station, just one of a stream of freight traffic that uses these lines.

Plate 75: Running towards Romford from Gidea Park, on 14th May 1982, No. 47568 heads the 15.46 Norwich to Liverpool Street service. The Class 47s have a long association with the ex-Great Eastern lines, as it was early in 1965 when they first commenced as motive power for the East Anglian services, and well into the 1980s before electrification was completed through to Norwich, allowing electric locomotives to power trains throughout.

Plate 76: The large BR logo and locomotive number adopted for some of the class from the early 1980s was amusingly referred to by many as the 'short-sighted engine spotters livery' and, it was true, the large bodyside numbers were an aid to identification of a fast moving train. On 14th May 1982, No. 47583 *County of Hertfordshire* storms through Harold Wood Station on the fast line with the 17.46 from Norwich to Liverpool Street working, and passes the 18.45 local service from Southend (Victoria) to the same destination, formed of two Class 307 electric multiple units, led by No. 101.

Plate 77: The 'down' 'East Anglian' express is taken through the Essex countryside, between Harold Wood and Brentwood, on 14th May 1982, by No. 47576, which is complete with a steam day's style headboard. This is one of the seven locomotives rostered for the Network SouthEast services to King's Lynn from May 1987, and painted in 'Network' livery. This one was named *King's Lynn* in January 1987.

Plate 78: On 1st June 1981, No. 47160 (47605) hammers through Whittlesford Station, south of Cambridge, with the 13.30 King's Lynn to Liverpool Street service and, for a few moments at least, tends to disturb the peace of the rural scene that is even complete with a wheelbarrow!

Plate 79: On 12th September 1983, No. 47571 climbs through Brantham, near Manningtree, with the 11.40 Norwich to Liverpool Street train, and passes tell-tale signs of the impending electrification, with trunking stacked in readiness against the bank.

Plate 80: On Belstead Bank, south of Ipswich, on the same day, No. 47093 powers a well-laden Freightliner service from Felixstowe to Stratford (London) Freightliner Terminal.

Plate 81 (Above): Passing Ipswich yards, and approaching East Suffolk Junction, north of the station, on 28th May 1981, No. 47580 *County of Essex* passes on time with the 14.30 from Liverpool Street to Norwich working.

Plate 82 (Above Right): Crossing the old Trowse swingbridge and the two-directional signal that once guarded it, No. 47138 (now 47607 *Royal Worcester*) hauls the 13.46 Yarmouth to Chesterfield service away from the environs of Norwich, on 10th September 1983.

Plate 83 (Right): Rounding the curve into Norwich Station on the same day, No. 47074 (47646) passes Norwich Thorpe Junction box with the summer Saturday 08.15 Manchester (Piccadilly) to Yarmouth service, a turn that often brought a Class 40 into East Anglia at this time.

Plate 84: The 'up' 'Day Continental' for Liverpool Street awaits for the ship from the Hook of Holland to dock at Harwich (Parkeston Quay) on 4th September 1981 before receiving any passengers. Motive power is provided by No. 47158 (47634) Henry Ford.

Plate 85: On the same day, No. 47117 is about to pass under the fine old signal gantry on the approaches to Parkeston Quay yards with steel from Llanwern in export containers. This was one of five locomotives of the fleet that bore the classification 48 when fitted with an experimental V12, single crankshaft engine from 1965 to the early 1970s.

New Lamps for Old

Plate 86: One has only to imagine travelling at speed in pitch darkness to appreciate that some form of headlight for locomotives was long overdue. Experimentally fitted with a type similar to the ones used for the Scottish push-pull services, No. 47574 (since named *Lloyd's List*) passes Old Milverton on the Coventry to Leamington Spa single spur, that used to include the station of Kenilworth, hauling a special 10.30 Wolverhampton to Paddington train, on 11th April 1981.

Plate 87: On 3rd September 1984, the same locomotive heads the 11.30 Liverpool Street to Norwich Inter-City service near Stratford and, despite many of the fleet at this time having been fitted with modern fixed beam lamps, is still carrying the original prototype.

Plate 88: The strangely-routed 08.05 Portsmouth Harbour to Poole, via Reading, train departs from Southampton on 4th September 1984 powered by No. 47265 (47591), one of few of the fleet remaining at this time with original type marker light panels. Running 'light engine' in the opposite direction is No. 47266 (47629), with a yellow surround to the headlights fitted in place of the marker lights, and with the current style fixed headlamp fitted off-centre below the panel.

Plate 89: At Old Oak Common Depot, on 25th February 1984, No. 47502 displays the newly acquired off-centre fixed beam headlamp, now standard for the fleet. This locomotive has since been converted for 'push-pull' operation, renumbered 47715, transferred to Scottish Region, and named *Haymarket*.

Plate 90: Faced with extremely dull conditions, the new headlamps can be a boon to the photographer and assist in providing a highlight in an otherwise very drab scene. With an exposure of 1/250th at f2, No. 47142 comes through Par Station, Cornwall, on 2nd October 1985, with loaded china clay hoods from Drinnick Mill to Lostwithiel. A storm is raging, the rain is torrential, and the sky is black.

Plate 91: A rare event occurred on 20th November 1984 when the Queen Mother travelled down the North Woolwich branch to open the Great Eastern Railway Musuem contained in the renovated buildings of the original North Woolwich Station. The 'down' journey was made behind steam locomotive *Flying Scotsman* and, as there are no turning facilities at the little terminus, Class 47/4 No. 47581 *Great Eastern,* in splendid condition, was utilised for the return to Stratford, (London).

Plate 92: The first locomotive of the fleet to be observed with the now standard headlamp was No. 47308, pictured on the freight only lines at Foxlow Junction, Staveley, Derbyshire, on 30th June 1983, with a haul of 'down' bogie tanks.

Plate 93: An unusual Class 47 working occurred on 25th May 1984 when No. 47226 arrived at the East Somerset Railway station and British Rail site of Cranmore. Trains of bitumen tanks regularly work to and from Cranmore and Ellesmore Port but, on this day, the special load was six 50 ton Procor wagons filled with stone ballast from Merehead Quarry, and needed by the preserved railway for their own tracks. Here the train contrasts beautifully with the gas lamps and bric-a-brac of the station.

John Vaughan

Plate 94: As the result of a failure with the rostered Class 50, Class 47/3 No. 47345 is pressed into service for hauling the 11.10 Waterloo to Exeter (St. David's) service on 14th July 1985, and passes the site of Nine Elms engine shed which is now New Covent Garden Market. In view of the time of year, the fact that the Part 3 members of the class have no train heating facilities should not cause any discomfort to the passengers.

Ken Brunt

Plate 95: The green Southern Railway signal box plate shows up clearly, as No. 47441 pauses at Yeovil (Pen Mill) Station on 1st September 1984 with the 16.00 Weymouth to Cardiff (Central) train. This service traverses the ridge of the Dorset Heights and then through rolling downland countryside, where stops are made at Dorchester West, Maiden Newton, Yeovil (Pen Mill), Castle Cary, Bruton, Frome and Westbury. It then passes through the beautiful wooded gorge of the Avon Valley, calling at Trowbridge, Bradford-on-Avon, Avoncliff, Freshford, Bath Spa and Bristol (Temple Meads), before proceeding to its destination, scheduled to be reached at 19.19 — a more than worthwhile journey for the scenery alone.

Plate 96 (Left): No. 47480 *Robin Hood* pounds through Reading (West) Station, on 14th June 1985, hauling the 09.00 cross-country service from Manchester (Piccadilly) to Poole.

Plate 97: Crossing the tiny River Yealm by way of the mighty Blachford Viaduct, east of Cornwood, near Ivybridge, on 12th July 1985, No. 47162 heads in the direction of Plymouth with an engineer's train. Following fire damage this locomotive was withdrawn in January 1987 in order to assist with the supply of spare parts, for others in the fleet.

Plate 98: On a sunny 3rd March 1984, No. 47453 speeds an attractive rake of Mk.II stock through the approaches to Barnt Green Station, forming the 08.25 Manchester (Piccadilly) to Cardiff (Central) service. The lines veering off to the left of the train are for the Redditch branch.

Plate 99 (Above): The 08.55 Penzance to Newcastle service arrives at Liskeard, Cornwall, on 2nd October 1985, hauled by No. 47602 *Glorious Devon*. The morning mist is clearing but there is not yet much light for photography as witness the glowing marker lights and headlamp.

Plate 101 (Above Right): On a wet 22nd November 1984, the 06.01 Derby to Brighton train prepares for the scheduled Gatwick Airport stop, having passed through Horley Station in the background. Again, with lights aglow, the train locomotive is No. 47613 *North Star,* one of the original batch of seventeen named by the Western Region in 1965.

Plate 100 (Left): A Holyhead to Willesden Freightliner service runs alongside one of the platforms of closed Manchester (Exchange) Station, on 31st May 1984, and approaches Manchester (Piccadilly) Station hauled by No. 47230. Prior to the fine old arched roof of Exchange being pulled down, this view was not possible.

Plate 102 (Lower Right): Very dull conditions are still apparent here as No. 47569 comes off the Cambridge lines at Bethnal Green, and joins the East Anglian main line into Liverpool Street, hauling the 12.20 train from Cambridge.

New Names and Old

Plate 103: The youngster's favourite. *Rail Riders,* the nameplate carried by No. 47406.

Plate 104: The original GWR style plate *Mammoth,* carried by No. 47653.

Plate 105: In addition to the plate *Great Eastern* No. 47581 also carries the Great Eastern Railway crest.

Plate 106: The Scottish Region nameplate *Sir Walter Scott,* attached to No. 47710.

Plate 107: The plate S.S. Great Britain, carried by No. 47508, and the plaque denoting that the locomotive was named by H.M. The Queen in 1985 as part of the 150th Anniversary of the Great Western Railway.

Plate 108: The City of Truro name-plate affixed to No. 47625 is cast in plain block capitals.

Plate 109: The GWR style nameplate Sir Daniel Gooch is seemingly secured to the body side of green-liveried No. 47628 by no fewer than 36 rivets. The GWR crest is also carried.

Plate 110: The 'standard' type of plate lettering, as shown on the cast alloy embellishment Stratford on No. 47007, but with a Great Eastern blue background in place of the usual red, and with Stratford's 'Cockney Sparrow' motif cast in metal. This locomotive, the first to receive a general repair at Stratford Traction Repair Shop, was named there on 15th November 1986.

Plate 111: Showing the standard placement for name-plates affixed to the Class 47 fleet is Windsor Castle, on the body side of current 'Royal' engine No. 47620 of Old Oak Common.

Midland Merry-go-Rounds

Plate 112: Empty merry-go-round coal hoppers hauled by No. 47322 pass Coalville, on the busy 'freight only' line between Burton-on-Trent and Leicester, on 1st July 1983, returning from Drakelow Power Station to Bagworth Colliery for refilling.

Plate 113: Loaded merry-go-round hoppers heading southwards are eased through Walsall Station, on 2nd March 1984, by No. 47278.

Plate 114: On the grey leap year morning of 29th February 1984, No. 47200 scampers down Hatton Bank with coal for Didcot Power Station. The Midlands coalfields are considered to be the best equipped in the country for merry-go-round operation with over 80 per cent output in the rapid-load category.

Plate 115: The basic principal of the merry-go-round coal train is for the near-continuous circuiting of the same set of hoppers from coal source to its place of consumption. Having deposited the load shown opposite, No. 47278 now returns through Ryecroft Junction, Walsall, to one of the Midlands collieries for reloading.

Plate: 116: As a BR Swindon Class 120 3-car diesel multiple unit passes, forming the 10.20 service from Crewe to Lincoln, on 1st July 1983, No. 47294 slowly completes the off-loading circuit of Willington Power Station, between Burton-on-Trent and Derby, and will shortly be released to collect another haul.

Plate 117: On the same day, No. 47369 takes the line for Rawdon Colliery at Moira West Junction with m.g.r. empty hoppers. One would have imagined that drivers would traverse the extensive subsidence that is apparent here with extreme caution but, in reality, the trains are taken through the switchback at a surprising speed and, seemingly, with complete disdain.

Plate 118: At Barrow Hill, north of Chesterfield, on 30th June 1983, No. 47372 heads south with fifteen loaded m.g.r. hoppers from one of the many coalfields that abound in this area.

Plate 119: With a 41A steam days style shed plate fixed just below the marker light panel, No. 47278 of Sheffield (Tinsley) Depot powers through Duffield, north of Derby, with a southbound evening m.g.r. train, on 27th June 1983. The 41A shed code, in steam days, in fact, denoted a Sheffield (Darnall) allocation.

Plate 120: With over thirty loaded m.g.r. hoppers in tow, No. 47322 passes Moira West Junction signal box, on 1st July 1983, heading for Drakelow Power Station. The single line to the left is the entry to Rawdon Colliery, and the lines diverging right are for Overseal Sidings.

Freightliners

Plate 121 (Left): With the spire of King's Sutton church in the background, a well-laden southbound Freightliner approaches Aynho Junction on the 'Birmingham direct' line, north of Oxford, on 8th May 1982, headed by No. 47188.

Plate 123 (Right): A Freightliner bound for Tilbury charges through Purfleet Station on 17th April 1984, hauled by No. 47191.

Plates 124 (Right): On a damp 8th November 1983, No. 47093 brings a charter Freightliner of Ford Motor Company containers from Halewood, Merseyside, through Stratford Station, where a fresh crew will take over for the final part of the journey to Harwich, (Parkeston Quay).

Plate 125 (Right): In teeming rain on 28th March 1984, a Freightliner for Southampton Maritime is powered through the soggy Hampshire countryside at Worting Junction, south of Basingstoke, by No. 47326.

Plate 122 (Left): On a sunny 23rd February 1985, No. 47373 hammers through Spondon, Derbyshire, with a Freightliner bound for Nottingham Freightliner Terminal.

Plate 126: An 'up' Freightliner stands in the loop at Fenny Compton, between Leamington Spa and Banbury, on 11th April 1981, headed by No. 47219, as No. 47529 passes hauling the 15.30 special from Wolverhampton to Paddington. Observe the neat looking front end of the nearest locomotive, with all semblance of the old marker light panel now removed.

Plate 127: Passing Western Junction signal box, Dalston Kingsland, on 15th October 1984, with a sparsely-laden Freightliner from Stratford, No. 47369 travels westwards via the North London line to its ultimate destination. At this time the line on the right led to Broad Street Station, from where the Richmond services operated.

Plate 128: A Freightliner from Dudley Freightliner Terminal heads northwards on the approaches to Walsall on 2nd March 1984, powered by No. 47440.

Plate 129: A train with a few containers, but consisting mainly of empty Freightliner flat wagons, is hauled through Ipswich East Suffolk Junction by No. 47572 on 12th September 1983, and heads for Felixstowe. This locomotive has since been put into Network SouthEast livery and named *Ely Cathedral.*

With the T.P.O.s

Plate 130: The 15.47 Travelling Post Office from Aberdeen departs from the 'Granite City' exactly on time, on 20th April 1982, headed by No. 47120, since named *R.A.F. Kinloss.* Passengers are allowed to be carried with this train and the two coaches to accommodate them are attached to the rear, and will terminate at Perth where the T.P.O. will be augmented before continuing south.
Plate 131: The 17.53 T.P.O. from Workington to Huddersfield stands at Lancaster Station on 8th February 1983, during loading. Traction is provided by No. 47419, which was withdrawn from service at Gateshead Depot on 11th February 1987 after sustaining fire damage.

Plate 132: All the Travelling Post Offices that once emanated from King's Cross Station have been transferred to St. Pancras and, during the hours of darkness, this station is probably the busiest in London. On 21st November 1985, No. 47491 *Horwich Enterprise* prepares to move the 22.25 T.P.O. for Newcastle northwards into the night. This locomotive was the 100th member of the class to be named.

Plate 133: A Travelling Post Office emanating from Derby and destined for the north is loaded in the station on the night of 20th February 1985, prior to its journey commencing. A mist is gathering and accentuates the headlight beam on No. 47608.

Plate 134: Class 47s are not constructed to work in multiple and, as such, instances of double-heading are not commonplace as two drivers are required, one in each locomotive. On 13th July 1985, however, a combined power of 5,160b.h.p. was considered necessary for haulage of the 11.32 Penzance to Manchester (Piccadilly) train, as both working members of the class, Nos. 47100 leading 47443, roar through Dawlish Warren Station.

Plate 136: On 5th February 1986, the 10.35 Oxford to Paddington train was double-headed by Nos. 47509 *Albion* and 47513 *Severn*. However, super power was not the order of the day as *Severn* was, in fact, 'dead'.

John Vaughan

Plate 135 (Below Left): Passing the Bristol suburb of Horfield with a rake of Ketton Cement Presflo wagons, on 8th June 1982, an active No. 47110 leads No. 47142, which has expired. It can be observed that the radiator grilles on the leading locomotive are wide open, whereas those on the other one are closed and out of use, being controlled by a thermostat.

Plate 137: Following the failure of Class 50 No. 50018 *Resolution* on the 16.15 Hereford to Paddington service, on 14th April 1985, Class 47 No. 47349 was sent to rescue the train. The last rays of the setting sun glint on the flanks of the two locomotives as they pass Old Oak Common well behind time.

Brian Beer

Speedlink Operations on the Western Region

Plate 138: A very mixed Speedlink service from St. Blazey heads eastwards near Lostwithiel, on 1st July 1980, with Presflo wagons dominant. The locomotive at this time, No. 47027, has since been fitted for electric train heating, consequently renumbered into the Section 4 category as No. 47558 and has also been named *Mayflower*.

Plate 139 (Above Right): An air-braked service freight from St. Blazey for Severn Tunnel Junction passes Cogload Junction, near Taunton, on 28th March 1985, powered by No. 47100. All Speedlink services are exclusively air-braked.

Plate 140 (Right): An 'up' Speedlink service freight passes Splottlands, Cardiff, on 9th June 1982, hauled by No. 47234. The train will, undoubtedly, be heading for Severn Tunnel Junction, which is one of the twelve main yards of the Speedlink network, and the only one on the Western Region; the others being Willesden, Bescot, Whitemoor, Toton, Doncaster, Healey Mills, Warrington, York (Dringhouses), Newcastle (Tyne), Carlisle and Glasgow.

Plate 141 (Left): No. 47015 passes between Bathampton Junction and Bath Spa Station, on 12th January 1983, with a short Speedlink haul of Rugby Cement Presflo hoppers and steel-carrying wagons.

Plate 142 (Below Left): Passing Norton Bavant, near Haytesbury, on the Western/Southern Region borders of the Westbury to Salisbury line, an unusual Speedlink service heads for Salisbury, consisting of No. 47236 leading Class 33/0 No. 33039, and hauling an armoured car on a flat wagon, an Esso tank, and one coal hopper! The Class 47 is in rather work-stained Railfreight livery.

Plate 143: No. 47353 passes the site of Brent Station, in South Devon, and the disused signal box, on 18th July 1985, with the morning Speedlink service from St. Blazey to Severn Tunnel Junction. The old Kingsbridge branch used to diverge from here, with the single track curving away from the main line just east of the station. The branch was closed in September 1963, leaving little reason for Brent Station to stay open, and closure systematically followed just thirteen months later.

Plate 144: A Speedlink service that consists, primarily, of cargo-wagons and slurry tanks passes the 'up' and 'down' holding loops near the summit of Hemerden Bank on the same day, hauled by No. 47293.

Stratford Interlude

Plate 145: A variety of Class 47 liveries are on show in Stratford depot yard on 16th January 1986, among which are shown No. 47582 *County of Norfolk,* in Inter-City sector livery, but un-named, No. 47487, and three other standard types. Some fifty of the fleet are usually allocated to this East London depot at any one time. *County of Norfolk* must have carried more paint styles than any other member of the fleet. As No. D1765 it was first painted in the original two-tone green, followed by standard blue when renumbered 47170. Stratford's home-made large logo livery followed, and then it was reverted to BR blue once again only to return again to a large logo style as No. 47582 when converted to electric train heating at BREL Crewe. Since this photograph was taken the locomotive has been repainted yet again in Network SouthEast's distinctive colours of red, white, blue and grey.

Plate 146: Inside Stratford's Traction Repair Shop (T.R.S.) on the same day, the inmates include No. 47520, with derailment damage to the bogies and awaiting lifting, No. 47542, having tyres turned, and No. 47406 *Rail Riders*, having rectifications undertaken to a fire alarm earthing fault.

Plate 147: Two Class 37s and six Class 47s are included in this view of Stratford T.R.S. photographed from the overhead crane.

Plate 148: Inside the main depot building at Stratford can be seen three of their allocation of the fleet, in typical and commendable condition. From left to right are Nos. 47583 *County of Hertfordshire*, 47569 and 47579 *James Nightall G.C.*

Single Line Workings

Plate 149: On 6th September 1984, No. 47197 trundles down the Hamworthy freight line to Poole Harbour with steel coil for export.

Plate 150: The 09.14 Weymouth to Temple Meads train approaches Castle Cary, on 1st September 1984, with No. 47061 (47649) providing traction. The Western Region line from Weymouth, that diverges from Southern Region metals at Dorchester West, is singled throughout.

Plate 151: On the 'freight only' line from Bletchley to Oxford, No. 47145 hauls empty stone hoppers from Bletchley stone terminal, and passes the disused signal box and station of Bicester (London Road), once a stop on the old Oxford to Cambridge LNWR line that closed in 1968. Twin tracks remained in situ until 1986 when singling commenced, as can be observed in this view photographed on 13th August of that year.

Plate 152: Complete with guard's van, the early morning 'company train' from Inverness to the B.A.C.O. smelter at Invergordon skirts the Inner Cromarty Firth on 20th June 1980, and can be said to be somewhat overpowered by No. 47427.

George C. O'Hara

Occasions

Plate 153: Adorned with steam age type headboard, and hauling the Steam Locomotive Operator's Association (S.L.O.A.) Pullman coaches, No. 47158 (47634) *Henry Ford* is in immaculate condition hauling the 'Flying Scotsman' special up Holloway Bank from Copenhagen Tunnel, on 27th February 1983.

Plate 154: On 25th and 26th September 1986, Nos. 47515 and 47549 were named *Night Mail* and *Royal Mail* respectively at Derby and St. Pancras. Dressed up in Inter-City livery for the occasion, No. 47549 prepares to leave St. Pancras, following the naming, with the 'Flying Postman' special. In the opposite platform Inter-City 125 power car No. 43118 heads the 11.15 for Nottingham.

Plate 155: Following the dry summer of 1983, and the resultant tendency for lineside fires, it was stipulated that all runs on British Rail metals by steam locomotives for a period would have to be undertaken in 'light steam', and hauled by a diesel locomotive. On 13th July 1983, No. 47491 (since named *Horwich Enterprise*) passes Chester racecourse with a S.L.O.A. special for Hereford. The rather belittled steam engine is 'Castle' Class 4-6-0 No. 5051 *Drysllwyn Castle*.

John Vaughan

Plate 156: On this occasion it is an Inter-City 125 unit forming the 13.36 Penzance to Paddington train that is belittled as, due to failure of one power car, it has to be assisted over the South Devon banks by No. 47279. The entourage is pictured here passing Powderham, near Starcross, on the South Devon coast, on 16th July 1981.

Plate 157: To commemorate the special issue of railway stamps released on 22nd January 1985, a 'Royal Mail' special, consisting of the V.S.O.E. Pullman set, ran from Paddington. The train locomotive is No. 47500 *Great Western,* which is seen passing between Nos. 47086 *Colossus* (now No. 47641 *Fife Region*) and 47625 *City of Truro.*

Plate 158: With the festivities in relation to the cross-London launch of Inter-City services on 9th May 1986 complete, one of the day's special trains departs from Kensington Olympia and heads guests back to Manchester (Piccadilly). No. 47487, in Inter-City Sector livery, took the train as far as Willesden, where an electric locomotive took over. The 'face' on the Class 47 matched the one used on the locomotive in the publicity material.

Plate 159: The first of the Class 47 fleet to be painted in Network SouthEast red, white, blue and grey livery was No. 47573 *The London Standard,* pictured here in Liverpool Street Station, on 9th June 1986, being serenaded following the naming ceremonies.

Plate 160: Another portent of the cross-London Inter-City services occurred on 11th January 1986, when No. 47408 *Finsbury Park* arrived at Newhaven Town Station with the 08.00 Brighton to Newhaven e.c.s. train prior to working the special 08.47 Newhaven to Manchester (Piccadilly) service, the line between Burgess Hill and Brighton being closed at the time. No. 47408 was one of the original twenty machines constructed in 1962 and which are now life-expired. Withdrawal took place later in the year and the name *Finsbury Park* has been transferred to No. 47654.

Trains in the Landscape

Plate 161 (Left): Hauling the 10.27 Paddington to Penzance train, No. 47110 winds through Lostwithiel Station, Cornwall, on 5th July 1984.

Plate 162: With Chesterfield's famous twisted church spire dominating the horizon, No. 47580 *County of Essex* leaves the station, following the timetabled stop, with the 07.17 Harwich (Parkeston Quay) to Manchester (Piccadilly) service on 4th September 1980. The train has since been extended to Edinburgh and Glasgow, and been given the title of 'The European'.

Plate 163: Amid typical Scottish scenery, between Aberdeen and Inverness, No. 47160 (47605) nears Insch with the six Mk.I coaches that make up the 11.52 train from the 'Granite City' to the Highland capital, on 17th April 1982.

Plate 164: With temperatures at Tebay that morning recorded as low as minus 20 degrees centigrade, the 9th February 1983 was positively a day for thermal underwear. With a block load of Ribble Cement Presflo hoppers, No. 47129 (47658) passes Greenholme, near Shap Fell, and heads south.

Plate 165: Just two days later, on 11th February 1983, the same bitterly cold weather prevails as No. 47224 rounds the bleak Cumbrian coast at Nethertown, hauling a Lakeland Colliery to Fiddler's Ferry Power Station m.g.r. coal train.

Plate 166: Scuttling through the Somerset countryside at Berkley, near Frome, on 16th April 1986, No. 47627 *City of Oxford* hauls the St. Blazey to Dover Polybulks that contain china clay for export.

Plate 167: On 6th September 1984, a Southern Region air-braked service freight from Eastleigh to Wool descends Parkstone Bank behind No. 47341 which, at this time, was allocated to Bescot.

Plate 168: On a dull 24th May 1980, No. 47413 skirts the mouth of the River Humber and approaches Cleethorpes with the 13.05 train from King's Cross. At this time the London to Cleethorpes services were more usually worked by one of the fleet of Class 55 'Deltics', the majority of which were withdrawn the following year.

Plate 169 (Below Left): Crossing Durham Viaduct, on 27th May 1980, No. 47422 slows for the station stop with the 11.45 Cardiff (Central) to Newcastle train.

47901

Plate 170: Prior to delivery to British shores of the Romanian-built Class 56 Co-Co diesel locomotives, a test-bed was needed to evaluate the Ruston-Paxman 16RK3CT power unit and other equipment that was contained in them. No. 47046 was in Crewe Works at this time for repair following accident damage, and was utilised for the purpose, being completely redesigned internally to take the new power unit, being fitted for train air-brake operation only, and receiving the new number 47601. Evaluation complete, the locomotive was again returned to Crewe to test the new 12RK3ACT Ruston-Paxman unit that was to power the new Class 58 fleet of Co-Co diesels that was then being developed and, to avoid a number clash with the ever-growing Class 47/4 e.t.h. conversion renumberings, was given its fourth cabside identification of 47901. The locomotive, which is now strictly a Type 5, is pictured here at Westbury Depot on 12th January 1983.

Plate 171: On 4th June 1984, No. 47901 hauls 43 loaded Yeoman stone hoppers from Merehead Quarry and traverses the Merehead branch, near Wanstrow, heading for Witham East Somerset Junction and the West of England main line.

Michael Mensing

Scotrail

Plate 172: With locomotive and train all in the attractive ScotRail livery of light and dark grey with blue and white stripe, No. 47704 *Dunedin* accelerates the 11.10 Glasgow (Queen Street) to Edinburgh push-pull service past the west end of Cadder Yard, between Bishopbriggs and Lenzie, on 26th April 1986. Standard headlamps have now replaced the original round spotlights that were fitted to the locomotives converted for push-pull operation in Scotland.

Tom Noble

Plate 173: On 18th March 1985, No. 47642 in ScotRail colours was a surprise visitor to Waterloo Station, London, with the 19.00 vans from Portsmouth & Southsea; the first ever appearance of the ScotRail livery to this station. In September 1986 this locomotive was given the name *Strathisla*.

Colin J. Marsden

Plate 174: No. 47712 *Lady Diana Spencer* heads the 13.34 Perth to Glasgow (Queen Street) service near Cadder Yard on 28th April 1986, the train comprising an Edinburgh to Glasgow push-pull set complete with the Driving Brake Open Second at the rear.
Tom Noble

Plate 175: The 14.00 Edinburgh to Glasgow (Queen Street) high speed push-pull train, with No. 47713 *Tayside Region* propelling, races through the West Lothian countryside between Croy and Lenzie on 29th April with DBSO No. 9703 leading. Observe the deflector plate now fitted to all of ScotRail's DBSOs following the fatal accident at Polmont on 30th July 1984, when a high speed train, being propelled, hit a cow and was derailed.
Tom Noble

Coats of Many Colours

Plate 176: With specially added paintwork embellishments in celebration of the wedding of the Prince and Princess of Wales, Stratford's No. 47583 *County of Hertfordshire* hammers through Whittlesford, south of Cambridge, on 28th July 1981, heading the 10.36 Liverpool Street to King's Lynn express.

Colin J. Marsden

Plate 177: With its grey Railfreight livery already becoming work-stained, No. 47374 (now named *Petrolea*) takes its turn with the Class 56s and 58s in moving coal from one of the various pits in the East Midlands to Didcot Power Station, on 5th February 1986. The train is leaving Aynho Park Junction, Oxfordshire, where it had been 'looped' to give precedence to a passenger train, and is passing what used to be the Aynho station building.

John Vaughan

Plate 178: With the Paignton 'branch' on the left, an 'up' vans train curves round the West of England main line at Aller Junction, south of Newton Abbot, on 12th July 1986, hauled by No. 47366 *The Institution of Civil Engineers,* in the livery of the Railfreight Sector with the addition of yellow cab roofs.

Plate 179: With a distinctive white stripe just below the level of the roof line applied by Thornaby Depot, No. 47308 passes Westbury on 16th April 1986 with the 13.10 Furzebrook to Llandarcy freight (6V37).

Plate 180 (Left): The first of the Class 47 fleet to be given the livery of Network SouthEast was No. 47573 *The London Standard*. Rostered for the 09.03 Wolverhampton to Dover (Western Docks) Inter-City service, on 15th June 1986, the splendid looking locomotive approaches Bromley South Station less than a week from the date of the Network SouthEast launch and its own naming ceremony, a part of which is illustrated in Plate 159.

Brian Beer

Plate 181 (Below Left): With newly applied large bodyside number and logo, wrap-around yellow front, black window surround and light grey roof, No. 47466 hauls the 07.15 Milton Keynes to Penzance Pullman service away from Newton Abbot on 12th July 1986, and approaches Aller Junction.

Plate 182 (Above): One of four Class 47s painted in GWR lined green livery for the 'GWR 150' commemorations, No. 47484 *Isambard Kingdom Brunel*, passes Ruscombe, near Twyford, on 3rd March 1986, with an air-braked service freight bound for Willesden. The other three locomotives similarly treated were *G. J. Churchward, Great Western* and *Sir Daniel Gooch*.

Colin J. Marsden

Plate 183 (Below): No. 47407 *Aycliffe* is unique among the Class 47/4 fleet in having the standard yellow painted front extended to include the cab roof. Standing in Paddington Station on 7th February 1985, after arrival with the 17.30 from Oxford, the locomotive also sports black window surrounds.

Plate 184: A number of the fleet allocated to Cardiff (Canton) Depot have the last three digits of the running number stencilled on the front, below the marker light panel, with this example also having received a matt black cab roof and window surrounds. On 18th June 1983, No. 47242 passes Beeston, on the outskirts of Leeds, with the 08.17 York to Tenby train.

John Vaughan

Plate 185 (Below): Another example of depot individualism is the treatment given by Sheffield (Tinsley) to No. 47374, with the last three digits of the number this time stencilled in white on the front portion of the cab roof. On 3rd July 1984, the locomotive hauls the 09.32 freight from St. Blazey to Severn Tunnel Junction and passes Worth, north of Exeter.

Plate 186 (Above Right): With West London office blocks forming the backcloth, No. 47490 rounds the curve approaching West Brompton, on 16th May 1986, having just restarted the 06.44 Manchester (Piccadilly) to Brighton Inter-City service from the Kensington Olympia stop.

Plate 187 (Below Right): On the same day, No. 47432 travels the West London line in the opposite direction with the 10.15 Brighton to Manchester (Piccadilly) train, and passes the rear of the Earl's Court complex on the left and Lillie Bridge London Transport depot on the right.

Plate 188: Both north to south and south to north cross-London Inter-City trains use the same platform at Kensington Olympia, and this often causes delays when services have scheduled stops there within a few minutes of each other. On 16th May 1986, the delayed 09.25 Manchester (Piccadilly) to Dover (Western Docks) train is restarted from the station by No. 47432. On the left, London Transport 'D' Stock forms the shuttle to and from High Street Kensington Station and, just visible on the centre road through the station, is the rear of a rake of stone hoppers powered by Class 56 No. 56061.

Plate 189: The 13.45 Dover (Western Docks) to Liverpool (Lime Street) Inter-City train passes through Kent's lush Sevenoaks Weald on 6th June 1986, powered by No. 47625 *City of Truro.*